The lounging lizard poet
of the floating world

BY KEITH HILL

POETRY
The Ecstasy of Cabeza de Vaca
Out of the Way World Here Comes Humanity!
Psalms of Exile and Return
The Bhagavad Gita: A New Poetic Version
I Cannot Live Without You:
Selected Poetry of Mirabai and Kabir
Interpretations of Desire:
Mystic Love Poems by the Sufi Master Ibn 'Arabi

FICTION
Puck of the Starways
Blue Kisses

NON-FICTION
The New Mysticism
The God Revolution
Striving To Be Human

The lounging lizard poet of the floating world

poems / antipoems

Keith Hill

First edition published in 2019 by Disjunct Books
Auckland, New Zealand

Paperback ISBN 978-0-9951204-8-8
Ebook ISBN 978-0-9951204-9-5

Copyright © Keith Hill 2019

Keith Hill's right to be identified as author of this work is asserted in accordance with Section 96 of the Copyright Act 1996.

All rights reserved. Except for fair dealing or brief passages quoted in a newspaper, magazine, radio, television or internet review, no part of this book may be reproduced in any form or by any means, or in any form of binding or cover other than that in which it is published, without permission in writing from the Publisher. This same condition is imposed on any subsequent purchaser.

Cover image: Ittoilmata / Shutterstock

Disjunct Books is an imprint of Attar Books, a New Zealand publisher focused on spiritually oriented literature. For more information on Disjunct Books' publications visit:

www.attarbooks.com

Warning

Stop! Think about it.
Do you really want to do this?
There's still time to close the book
discretely return it to the shelf
and go back the way you came ...

Contents

What the poet had to say during
his apprenticeship   11

Since then . . .

Declaration   15
Literature vs the antipoem   18
What is an antipoem?   21
The modern dilemma   22
Confessions of a labour unit   27
Instructions for modern living
    1. How to become superexcited   31
    2. The impact of being superexcited   32
    3. Countering being superexcited   33
How to succeed in business   34
Instagram profundities   39
2001: I would like to meet you   40

The lounging lizard poet of the floating world

The lizard poet   49
Poetry   50
Identity   51
Funny   52
Communication   53
Talkback   54
Future   55

Survivor	56
Burgers	57
Mystery	58
Water	59
Deal	60
Platform	61
Daiquiri	62

Meanwhile . . .

Memoir	65
Coda	77
2018: They made it fun	80
The poet as agony aunt	89
Post-mortem	99

Acknowledgements

References	103
A Tribute	107
Remembering Nicanor Parra	108
To the reader	109

Dedication

Let's get this collection on the road. Yet the road being murky, at best, and the poet having his arse on backwards—which results in the peculiar gait revealed in these pages—by way of an opening dedication the best that can be done is to thank Gregory Richards and Trevor Dobbin who, during the poet's youth, opened windows that revealed impressive artistic vistas, then urged him to jump. When he hesitated, the apprentice received added impetus from Nicanor Parra, who kicked him out the window onto the road, threw down paper and a pen, and offered this advice:

In poetry everything is permitted.

With only this one condition, of course:
You have to improve on the blank page.

What the poet had to say during his apprenticeship

Life has many forces
so many cardboard tubes rolling in all directions

The poet looks out the moving train's window
contemplating the camels running in the gutter
as he attempts to direct himself
at the clouds moving across the sky
he writes a poem about it

The apprentice has plenty to amuse himself with
but consistently he is fascinated by women
the one who laughed at everything
the one whose eyes ran across him like lizard's feet
the one who said she'd love to be a virgin
all these walked past the apprentice
and he wondered what their names were

But other activities demanded his attention
violins played all night
he became trapped in long monologues with old men
people jumped out on him from behind bushes
he was asked to describe an acorn
so he found himself waltzing when he wanted to walk
and only the dust to sustain him

He laughed when everyone else laughed
he talked non-stop for six days
to no avail
until one day he saw the brick walls

on the horizon and decided to direct
his movements to resolve contradiction
But let's ask the poet what he thought
of these progressions
   ... with the speed of a spaceship
         flashing its snapshot eyes ...

[Written in 1975]

Since then . . .

Declaration

Let me begin by welcoming
not just our most honourable
ladies and gentlemen
but all who cannot be pinned down
by either-or genderising
have never worn a badge that denoted
them as honourable or needing respect
and whose presence cannot
unambiguously be assigned a page
in the encyclopedia of identity—
to all these I offer a declaration.

Life is not an omp-pah-pah band
marching round a train station
while ushers hand out dance cards.
Life is not a spectacle that conforms
to Hollywood three-act structure
in which your story happily resolves
moments before the director yells cut.
Life is not a blip on a screen
that experts solemnly measure
record notate and theorise over
which then fizzes into nothingness
when they switch off the lights
and go home for dinner.

I know you know this is not news
because you have lain in the dark
watching your life swim across the ceiling.

You have wondered whether the bungy cord
that connects you to the world
is ultimately tethered to anything.
You have felt your stomach lurch
before your feet leaped.
You have barked at the moon
in the middle of a traffic jam
and heard the moon howl back.

In response to these conundrums
let me now most solemnly declare
you will find in these pages
no special revelations.
If you have come seeking equations
that show the balance of good and evil
in another's soul (or your own)
you have ticked the wrong box.
If you want to dissect your life
to find exactly where it was
you took that confusing turn
you are holding the wrong instrument.
If you want to learn to survive while
balancing the future on your nose
you will need to select force quit.

The poet is not a regurgitator of half
truths that promise the world
but just cha-cha round the dentist's chair.
The poet is not a speed camera
spitting out reports each half hour.
The poet is not a piano solo performed
on an airport runway among synchronised

cheerleaders who toss burning batons while
screeching jumbo jets plant tyre marks
across the applauding passengers' hopes.
No. I take that back.
The poet *is* a piano solo
a crash landing
a lightning conductor
a siren on roller skates
a wild tipster handing out dance cards
an accident waiting for the opportunity
to happen.

Accordingly all I can promise is that
I will look behind the mirror and
celebrate what is living back there ...
draw a diagram on a handkerchief
that dazzlingly illuminates
how inside and outside connect ...
lob an antipoem through the window
of the adjudicator of the literary awards
then wait for whatever comes back ...
open the door in your shadow
that sends us all skidding unstoppably
into the void ...

Literature vs the antipoem

Literature like most things is
best taken in moderation.
What else to take in moderation?
Education marriage childbirth
holidays politicians ice cream
advice hesitation future plans
and a life as a poet.

It may be claimed literature
is instinctively moderate.
It patiently waits for months
in a bookcase or on that far shelf
until it is finally acknowledged
and given permission to open up.
It then eloquently evokes a memory
offers an urbane metaphor
or tells an engaging story
designed to make readers frown smile
or nod their head in recognition.
The rules of literature dictate works
must be soundly structured.
That they be written with attention to
the power of words needs no comment.
Note that giving voice to the darkness
which murmurs in the human heart
has proved adept at seducing
literary critics and award judges.
But remember to use theatrical blood.
Real blood is an inconvenience

as it splatters face and clothing
and refuses to vanish the moment
the book is shut.

In contrast the antipoem is immoderate.
It doesn't know its place
and is never shapely or urbane.
The antipoem has not been dipped
in the troughs of good taste
and so lacks the laminated sheen
that marks literary excellence.
Consequently a reeking smell may cling to
the antipoem as it steps onto the page
making it necessary to hold one's nose
when reading a particularly pungent passage.
What of the claim the antipoem is a bully
who when invited to public events
boots well-crafted verses off the stage
and threatens violence if it hears "just one
more line of fucking iambic pentameter"?
Are antipoems a threat to the silken
existence of demure poems
in whose mouths literature doesn't melt?
Do antipoems pick their teeth
with the bones of tepid poems
whose word-flesh dissolves when exposed
to one of their particularly odious yawns?
All these are exaggerations generated
by those who fear rippling the pond
yet long for the frog to be a prince.
The judgement of those who suspect
antipoems have themselves spread fake news

overstating their subversiveness
out of childish look-at-me pique
is either an expression of jealousy
or is correct.

The antipoem may be uncouth
but it is not perverse.
Think of it as an unschooled cousin recently
arrived from the far side of the mirror
who has never learned how to bow a tie.
This is why the antipoem walks
           .sdrawkcab
Examples include pulling hats out of rabbits
following in the footsteps of your shadow
and describing the plight of those
who have died before they were born.
The antipoem remains friendly as long as
it is not approached front-on.
Best practice is to sidle up as it watches you
out the corner of its eye.
Yet antipoems party as hard as literary poems.
An antipoem may on occasion even
hold hands with a poem
perhaps on the back porch drunk and disorderly
or when they climb a wall together
to escape the frustrations of modern life.
As for the intriguing question of who
their baby would look like
that may only be answered by midwives
undertakers literary critics and those
who shoot like a rocket towards the moon.

What is an antipoem?

An antipoem is icecream
in a cone balanced on its sharp tip
on the road to Bulawayo
on the hottest day of the year
that stubbornly refuses to melt.

An antipoem is a shadow
that decides to take the day off
books an Uber hops a plane
and ends up in the Himalayas
posting blank selfies of the view.

An antipoem is a baby
that doesn't want to be born
but when it finally arrives
it's smoking a cigar and making
plans for the coming devolution.

An antipoem is a ticking book
delivered to the Ministry for Culture
but after the bomb squad
blows it up they only find cogs
from 14 wind-up sonnets.

An antipoem is an invitation
to a wedding where the mothers-in-law
are smirking the best man won't say
what's happened to the bride
the celebrant has drunk the champagne
and no one believes in marriage anyway.

The modern dilemma

Having spent a lifetime of Western privilege
doing the limbo while jumping over my knees
I feel it is my right now to proclaim
I consider myself short-changed.
During hours spent stopped in rush hour queues
I have meticulously catalogued the disparities
between what people heap on their teaspoons
and the unnamed ghouls that slink
past their windows at night.
I will try to keep it short.
But there is no way to make it pretty.

I begin by stating the obvious.
Everyone is so distracted by abstract nouns
—democracy religion economics freedom
biology sexuality orientation identity
status fashion novelty literature—
they don't notice what is really going on.
I refer to the modern process
by which the machinery of civilisation
inserts a straw into the brain
extracts the juices
then pounds what is left to form
an attitude an identity a reputation a career.
In the face of this provocation continuing
to chew gum is clearly inadequate.
So is becoming overexcited.
That stars light up and fade away
the sun rises and sets

people are born live or don't live then die—
these are unshakeable facts.
Better to resolutely face what is
than salivate over the dream of driving
the world's latest blancmange automobile.

You may ask what denotes what is.
This is a question much debated within
the hallowed halls of the academy
where grids and rules are imposed on thought
requiring copious references and quotations
(each meticulously footnoted)
to ensure all answers remain safely within
the bounds of what is already known.
As for everyone else
at birth we are each supplied with
an assortment of approved answers
concocted by theologians social Darwinists
businessmen politicians pugilists
thespians cynics narcissists
and that aunt with a wicked sense of humour.
Having adopted an explanation
(fabricated from the finest abstract nouns)
we then cling to it for a lifetime
hoping it will save us from the worst.
I note one exception which
consists of those who stand on tiptoes
attempting to pluck the moon from the sky.

How do you stop the juice being
extracted from your brain?
This is another question on which

there is no agreement.
Some consider such questions a category error
arguing being overwhelmed with doubt
has for too long been misconstrued
as evidence human beings possess a soul.
Others use the age-old smallness thesis
the modern version of which claims
we are only a glint of light on a sliver of DNA
so how could we dream of embracing the sun?
Yet others petition the ancient prophets' God
who wrote all his bestsellers millennia ago
and has long since succumbed to writer's block.
It may be surmised the many other gods
who once presided over our kneeled forebears
have their own reasons for no longer sending
missives from beyond.
This has left modern humanity perplexed.
We are each now a troubled mind staring out
through the sockets in our endoskeleton
eyes roaming like searchlights
across the bumps and crevices of the world.
Only the undaunted few dare look down to
observe their toes hanging over the ledge
below which yawns the precipice
that separates life from death.
This is not a sight for beginners.

As for the ghouls who haunt the night
best to leave them in the basement.
Undisturbed they happily get drunk
play video games and watch football.
But if interrupted they easily anger

and may kick down the door
jump out through your eyes and start
tossing furniture round the living room.
Worst is when groups of ghouls gather
in the streets and start partying.
The smell of burning often follows.
Then good people are required to gather
their allotment of generosity and calm
throw them into a blender
and share a humanising smoothie with those
who spend their nights high in cellphone towers
terrified of the ghouls baying below
and sobbing as they desperately call people
they're not sure how to talk to.
All this in a civilisation that considers itself
the greatest in human history!

A word of warning to the young.
You may be tempted to disobey your parents
climb out the bedroom window
and walk the streets until dawn
seeking fulfilment through adventure.
Wanderlust is natural when growing up.
But be wary of mirrors.
In particular do not stop and stare so long
into store windows you start to see yourself.
You risk being sucked in and
no one ever hearing from you again.

Regarding the many other awkward issues
that trouble us today such as
why we abruptly wake sweating at night ...

what that burning smell is we sometimes
notice in the middle of the day ...
how come no matter how long we walk
our soul is jerked back to where it started ...
why we can't reach up and touch the moon ...
these are questions for which each
must find their own answers.

Confessions of a labour unit

Let's be clear from the beginning.
A poet is not a viable economic unit.
I always knew walking on my hands
would lead to fascinating insights
but I never expected to make money.
No. What upset me was everything else.
Even then I understood nothing.

Human life involves a series of steps
that progress us year by year
along the path from birth to death.
As occurs to all the young
I was fed into the education machine.
Years later it spat me out
my forehead stamped to designate me
an approved member of society.
Next I was required to become economical.
I soon discovered this is more complex
than such a simple command implies
given the modern world is
hugely economical with facts and feelings
regarding the nature of human exchange.
I had long been assured I would be amply
rewarded if I put my shoulder to the wheel
and contributed my fair share.
Others claimed doing so is to become a naive
cog in a vastly manipulated roller coaster.
A savvy few offered courses on how to exploit
the opportunities roller coasters present

and eventually be crowned a lord of industry.
For those possessing no business acumen
an alternative path to fortune was offered
of becoming a celebrity roller coaster rider.
These choices just left me bewildered.

Poet not being a recognised category
in the nation's official register of employment
I was encouraged to "be practical"
and ride one of the waves of work
generated by revolving roller coasters.
It transpired this involved adopting
a work practice dating back to medieval times
of serfing the economy.
I took this instruction very seriously.
For years I tried jump-starting a career
diligently applying hair jel and toothpaste
and wearing a special smile I reserved for big
occasions like sitting shoulder to shoulder
with strangers on public transport
attending literary gatherings
and standing in front of firing squads.

Some initiates who had insights into
the secrets of being economical
tried dissolving my confusion
by praising mathematical modelling.
Where the medieval priest once preached
a metaphysical model in which our soul
is situated somewhere in the mutually
exclusive zones of heaven earth and hell
today's economist models our future

using a Venn diagram that shows the sweet spot
where savings stocks and investments intersect.
Foolishly I joked this was like constructing
a mathematical model for poetic creation
and claiming it could predict the words
a poet will use twenty years from now.
In response I was informed what would
quite predictably happen if
I did not treat being economical seriously.
This threat was not made to me alone.
Those who oversee our lives require us all
to deferentially clip the hedges
that line the paths we civilly walk along
on our journey from birth to death
and to politely pause when important men
their shoulders draped with overcoats
helicopter above us into private estates
where they land behind iron gates
to play golf drink whiskey
and decide our collective future.
Naturally this is a contentious topic
only discussed by suspect intellectuals
socialists conspiracy theorists
and poets way out of their depth.
No wonder for years I felt
I was waltzing when I wanted to walk!

Seeking solutions to being confused
is like trying to control the modern
population drift from churches to bars.
Those who have analysed the situation
propose that instead of banging our heads

against immovable iron gates
an acceptable alternative
is to buy a new blender television or phone.
This won't change our circumstances.
But at least then we have something.

Instructions for modern living

1. How to become superexcited

Salivate over the opportunity to buy the latest model phone
    the day it goes on sale.
Join the exclusive million watching Busy Philipps do her
    daily workout on Instagram Stories.
Push to the stage front at a Lorde concert and make eye
    contact as she sings just to you.
Do LA's Celebrity Homes Tour to see where Katy Perry
    lives then hang out later to spot whoever is inside.
Take a selfie in the lobby of that awesome Dubai hotel
    where *[insert your favourite celebrity]* stayed last year.
Make plans with friends to group book a Moon trip on
    Virgin Galatic to celebrate your birthday.
Persuade your lover to train their pubic hair into a
    bandito's moustache for Movember.
Follow *[insert your favourite superstar]* and share the amazing
    insights you get into their life.
Slam in a Twitter storm the trolls who mock the superstar's
    contribution to the world.
Slut-shame on their Facebook page the bitch who stole
    your lover at that party that sucked anyway.
Regain your cool by hitting the credit card in that amazing
    new mall with your new BFF.

2. The impact of being superexcited

Your eyes constantly look down and your arm jerks to rhythms generated by taps swipes deletes sends.
You enter alleys where vaping avatars exhale ones and zeros only readable by the glow of your phone.
Your mind becomes a hot air balloon bobbing in datastreams produced by jets of gushing digital media.
Your feet balance precariously on tightropes woven from celebrities' shares.
You are plagued by dreams that battery failure will interrupt your life's totally unreal upward curve.
Your adrenal glands become so hyper-extended you have to hide them by sharing photos of you aged ten.
You wake from nightmares of being lost in the galleries of data mines carved out by marketeers.
Your soul starts losing weight as your online metadata is repeatedly sold to whoever will pay.
You realise you live in a cage of algorithms created by coders chained to their desks by ghouls.
You attempt to reclaim your existence by writing a virtual autobiography you create one upload at a time.
Prowling ghouls become so demanding your shadow goes into hiding and you lose all sense of who you are.

3. Countering being superexcited

Stare for an hour into a mirror while resisting the urge to check your phone.
Leave your desires in a supermarket car park with the driver's door open and key in the ignition.
Select twelve words you consider crucial to your existence and randomly swap their meanings.
Walk backwards down the street so for the first time you can see where you have been.
Stand in front of a door repeatedly locking and unlocking it until the wall dissolves.
Sit quietly for a period each day to allow your shadow time to catch up.
Carry an alternative identity in your pocket which when life gets too intense you can unfold and step into.
Hang round in malls asking awkward questions until you get arrested for impersonating a human being.
Make a list of what you find and put out a media release that licks people when they lean in.
Walk to the top of that hill to check out the amazing view then keep walking.
Ensure that when you make a noise it is more meaningful than remaining silent.

How to succeed in business

Establish an insurance company.
Sell truckloads of premiums.
Wait for an earthquake.
Relax by attending cocktail parties.
After the earthquake
release a media statement
affirming it is a catastrophe
so many have lost their homes and
your company's goal is to support
all policy holders to ensure
they get their previous lives back
as soon as humanly possible.
Invite your insurance colleagues
to a working cocktail party
and devise a business strategy
sensitive to the situation.

Support the establishment
of a new government agency
to coordinate business and local
and national government efforts
to assure distraught home owners
that rebuilding will employ
a joined-up approach that begins
as fast as humanly possible.
When the newly appointed agency
recommends a claims process
that matches your business plan
release a media statement

approving it as the logical structure
and a big win for distraught owners.
Order vermouth and olives.

Add up liabilities on all policies
then transform the claims process
from the cost of doing business
into a profit centre.
To achieve this smoothly
give government and bureaucrats
the two years they need to stand
all their ducks in a row
to create a sound rebuild process.
Invite tenders from call centres
around the world to ensure
your clients always have available
someone knowledgeable
to discuss the details of their claim.
Choose a country where the operators
speak English well enough and follow
your coaching forms excellently.
Have lawyers write the coaching forms
to ensure claimants' contracted rights
are respected and expedited efficiently
within the legally enforceable terms.
Buy cases of vermouth olives and gin.
Learn how to mix martinis.

Speak to local media to assure
distraught home owners your company
wants them to get back their normal lives
as soon as humanly possible.

Employ assessors who are able to
speed up the process by pointing out
current damage that can be claimed
and historic damage that cannot.
Have the government agency
employ its own damage accessors.
Expect them to contradict each other.
Encourage owners to employ their own
assessors and inform them it is their right
to challenge all assessments in court.
Persuade the agency to persuade
the minster to persuade government
to persuade policy holders this
is their best hope for getting
everyone's ducks in a row.
Import an award-winning Filipino
barman to mix your colleagues' cocktails.
Drink an awful lot of martinis.

Invite tenders from builders.
To ensure all owners have equal access
to stretched insurance company funds
put a cap on each rebuild's cost.
Allow government to take the lead
in low-balling proposed quotes as
they are using tax-payer funds to top
up insurance pay-outs and optics
require them to be fiscally conservative.
After the minister has announced this
invite him to a business meeting and
fill him with award-winning martinis.

Begin distributing insurance pay-outs.
Have managers assess the risks
on payments and establish a bell curve
that extends one to ten years.
Situate claimants along the curve.
Ensure the first rebuild owners
appear exultantly on national television
arm-in-arm with their happy builders.
Graduate from martinis to screwdrivers.

Develop a strategy to deal with claimants
on the distant end of the pay-out curve.
Ensure local executives are not accessible
as contact will unnecessarily distract
policy holders from their primary task
which is to rebuild their home and life.
Stay away from local supermarkets.
If you inadvertently meet a claimant present
compassion but not your business card.
Send a representative to a public meeting
to ensure policy holders know their lives
are important and they are being heard.
Have him hear their stories filled with
frustration angst anger fear depression.
Tell your representative to assure policy holders
you intend to return their lives to normal
as soon as is humanly possible.
Be neither shaken nor stirred.

With the delayed pay-out monies now
sitting idle establish an equity fund and

explore new business opportunities—
underwriting Canadian pipeline construction
bottling Greenland freshwater glacial melt
marketing venereal treatments in the Congo
promoting eco-friendly rain forest removal
backing Australian tourism by building a
plastic replacement Great Barrier Reef.
Return home in time for duck shooting season.

When the first rebuilders become distraught
because their repairs are found to be faulty
regretfully inform policy holders
you are unable to respond in person
but you have faith in the minister
and his agency's processes so will
defer to governmental judgement.
Learn to mix Harvey Wallbangers.
Do it as fast as humanly possible.

Instagram profundities

When your house is lapped by water due to sea level rise should backstroke or breaststroke be preferred?

People say education is wasted on the young but isn't it foisted on them because no one else wants it?

When did it become best practice to persuade a country's leaders to change tack by torturing its population?

What identity can really be created from clicks collected by search engines and collated by algorithms?

If computer chips double capacity every 18 months why do we still use combustion engines invented 200 years ago?

When discussing big issues do people prefer to shoot from their hip because it's closest to their arse?

Does your left hand only start telling your right hand what it is doing when both are tied behind your back?

Is poetry a tough sell because while it may be the song of the soul who wants to be reminded they have a soul?

Write your answers on a postcard and toss it without ceremony into the void.

2001: I would like to meet you

It's hard to miss them.
The epitome of casual geek chic as
—organised within the warranty
of their Palm Pilots—
they sip labour-intensive cafe lattes
chat on sleek cellphones
and ponder the road to enlightenment.
They are bourgeois bohemians or Bobos
and they're the new enlightened elite
of the information age.

"My son wasn't a gangster"
says Eherta Selassie-Tikur
whose eldest son Affa
was found floating in a canal
with four bullets in the back of his head.
He was twenty-one.

Want to know how to acquire
a brand new residential investment
property for $15,000 to $240,000
that has a guaranteed lease
to a blue-chip corporate entity
generates extraordinary tax benefits
has freehold title
and is so hassle free
my biggest decision is where
you want the cheque sent each month?

Nearly one-third of Americans
toiling at low-wage jobs
cannot afford rent healthcare
or even enough food
says a liberal policy group.
One panellist presenting the study
author Barbara Ehrenreich
tested life at the poverty line
and found it impossible to live
on the minimum wage as a maid
waitress or Wal-Mart shop assistant.

    Wanted. A good male buddy
    for a mum 32 and her son 5.
    If you can have fun like a kid
    and also be a nice adult
    (at the right times!)
    please reply.

According to official British records
Idi Amin the brutal dictator who ruled
Uganda from 1971 to 1979
was virtually bone from the neck up
and needed things explained in words
of one letter.
Aside from that he was a splendid type
and a good rugby player.

Green fingered British prisoners
scooped a coveted Royal Horticultural Society
gold award at the Chelsea Flower Show
with their garden Time the Healer.

The prisoners serving time for offences
including fraud and assault
were allowed out on day release
for three weeks to complete the back-
breaking work of bedding in the plants.

A man who objected to government
inspections of his sausage factory
was in custody yesterday
after allegedly shooting
three inspectors to death
and chasing a fourth with a gun.
A friend Michael Smith said
"He was a good man but pressure
pressure
everyone blows up under pressure."

A special jail wing in India's capital
for mothers-in-law arrested for demanding
excessive dowry and breaking up marriages
faces overcrowding due to the pressure
of too many new entrants.
A majority of the mothers-in-law claimed
to be innocent victims of the evil
mechanisations of their wily
daughters-in-law who successfully
duped their guileless sons into
conspiring against them.

Need to brush up on the fine art
of composing ransom notes?
How about advice on choosing

a kidnapping victim?
A Brazilian school promised to teach
you all that in several easy lessons
until police raided the institution.
Police said student assignments
included the abduction of 64 people
in the past 2 months in Sao Paulo.
Police arrested 4 students and
are seeking their instructors.

Call it another giant leap for mankind.
Celestis Inc is now taking bookings
to bury the dearly departed on the moon
as early as next year.
"We want to open the space frontier
for everyone" said co-founder Charlie Chafer.
"The funeral industry is changing.
Baby boomers want to do things
a little differently."

A mentally ill deaf man spent nearly
2 years in jail before anyone realised
he didn't belong there.
Heard 42 spent the time inside a solitary cell
in the jail's mental health unit.
Unable to hear or speak he tried
to communicate his plight in notes he passed
to doctors and nurses but they threw them away.
"Isolation was the hardest"
said Heard through an interpreter.
"TV kept me going and I held the hope
I would be free one day."

Attractive sensuous 40s
lady seeks that rare gem
of a man mature but
useful romantic soh
with good looks
and that special x-factor.
You could be what's
missing from my life.

In 1999 no region on Earth was spared
as deadly conflicts ignited around the globe
and almost two-thirds of the world's nations
were accused of human rights abuses
Amnesty International said in its annual report.
Cases of summary execution were recorded
in at least 38 nations the detention of
"prisoners of conscience" in 61 countries
and torture in 132.

The Australian Centre for Mystery Investigation
the only national database for strangeness
has released the Weird Index
for the 1999–2000 financial year revealing
a national increase in the unusual of 13 per cent.
It builds on 5 consecutive years of growth.
The winner of the prestigious
Tim the Yowie Man Award for
"the most bizarre act of ineptitude or stupidity"
was a young man in Northern Territory.
Described as a worthy winner
the gentleman proposed to his girlfriend
by swinging Tarzan-style into her bedroom

window from a nearby telegraph pole.
Sadly the window was shut
and his almost bride-to-be rejected his offer
as he lay in hospital recovering from his injuries.

In 2025 US aerospace forces can own
the weather by capitalising on emerging
technologies and focusing development of
those technologies to war applications.
Such a capability offers the war fighter
tools to shape the battlespace
in ways never possible before.
While some segments of society will always
be reluctant to examine controversial issues
such as weather modification
the tremendous military capabilities that
could result from this developing field
are ignored at our peril.
[From *Owning the Weather in 2025* presented in
1996 by 7 high-ranking officers to the USAF]

A self-confessed Nazi who killed three people
in a spate of nailbombings across London
found bomb-making a form of therapy
a psychiatrist told a British court yesterday.
David Copeland 24 has pleaded guilty
to 3 bombings which injured
more than 100 people
and to 3 counts of manslaughter
on the grounds of diminished responsibility.
Dr Philip Joseph told Britain's top
criminal court at the Old Bailey

Copeland was not psychotic but
an anxious person who used bombing
to give his life meaning.

> Tall lady 3.30pm on 1 May.
> I was driving a red Ford
> stopped for you and you
> looked at me several times.
> You then walked on to
> the nearby fitness centre.
> I would like to meet you.

The lounging lizard poet
of the floating world

The lizard poet

The lizard poet is an observer floating languidly
on the detritus of a once great civilisation.

The lizard poet looks at the passing world
through giant unblinking reptilian eyes.

The lizard poet darts a forked tongue to sniff
each moment and promises to talk straight.

The lizard poet rolls up past and future
and uses them to snort the present.

The lizard poet projects his images on the retina
of a world that has its mind tight shut.

The lizard poet blows smoke rings and within each
creates the world in his own reptilian image.

The lizard poet flaps his lips like a magic carpet
to rhapsodise on the state of ... whatever.

Poetry

The poet champs at the start gate inspiration
at the ready excitedly waiting the gun.

The poet is a thoroughbred in a world
dedicated to putting the cart before the horse.

The poet launches his talent over rails set up
on a track he is uniquely equipped to run.

The poet loves feeling his muscles pump and
the sensation of flying through the air.

The poet is simultaneously in the stand savouring
the smells and the hooves' thump on the grass.

The poet's secret is being committed to the race
while chasing butterflies and watching clouds.

The poet gallops past the finish line cameras
bolts up the hill and vanishes over the horizon.

Identity

The raconteur is happiest leaning on the bar
introducing others to the people he used to be.

The raconteur has a story for every person a lover
in every story and a laugh or a sob for each ending.

The raconteur doesn't so much reinvent personal history
as adjust it to match the duration of the bar tab.

The raconteur tosses his identity into a laughing group
in exchange for someplace welcoming to be.

The raconteur sometimes wakes up not feeling himself
but puts it down to that last chaser after midnight.

The raconteur checks himself in the mirror as he shaves
marvelling so many people can share one face.

The raconteur reboots himself at five each afternoon
as he enters a bar to meet the next after-work crowd.

Funny

The cartoonist sits at the peak of 14 billion years
of evolution but can't find anything to watch on TV.

The cartoonist walks from the couch opens the fridge
and cracks another bottle of their favourite beer.

The cartoonist wonders if other beings like them are
doing the same on another planet in another galaxy.

The cartoonist ponders whether that planet creates
entertainment that beams straight into the cortex.

The cartoonist marvels natural selection has evolved
cognitive functions that facilitate infinite insights.

The cartoonist theorises the next phase of evolution
will lead to transrational interdimensional perceptions.

The cartoonist smells the smoke drifting from that
day's headlines and sits to sketch tomorrow's funny.

Communication

The pundit bungy jumps into the yawning gap
between what people say and what they think.

The pundit fossicks in the attic and discovers
not a lot of thinking is going on up there.

The pundit pulls out biases hidden in boxes the
owners claim are only opened once in a blue moon.

The pundit realises to relate to his era he needs to
spend more time communicating and less thinking.

The pundit starts a hugely communicative blog that
has one request—you tell me what's *really* going on.

The pundit concludes humanity is an unanswered
question people walk past their entire lives.

The pundit intended to end on something profound
but was diverted by that other whatever it is.

Talkback

The talk host agrees the purpose of democracy is to
protect the rights of the wealthy to become wealthier.

The talk host insists instead of dissing tax dodgers
we should set up our country as a tax haven too.

The talk host laments those holding out their tongues
to capture trickle down aren't sufficiently grateful.

The talk host argues for commonsense solutions
in a world where people want to be mollycoddled.

The talk host suggests the way to deal with too many
potholes on public roads is to buy a helicopter.

The talk host knows so any opportunities are out there
only the lazy complain they can't afford a helicopter.

The talk host has such rapport with his listeners his
toughest decision is deciding which helicopter to buy.

Future

The speculator acknowledges world peace is a great goal but argues first someone has to kill all the bad guys.

The speculator knows we need to strategise for sea level rise but only after he sells his waterfront timeshare.

The speculator agrees we have to wean off hydrocarbons so shifts his share portfolio from oil to armaments.

The speculator feels like a prophet without a country given his fellow citizens don't see the amazing opportunities.

The speculator sets up a company to sell land for hideouts to spooked tech billionaires prepping for Armageddon.

The speculator wants to shake the country and convince it everyone would profit from selling off New Zealand.

The speculator regrets people fixate on themselves when what's epic is signing a deal on a speedboat in Queenstown.

Survivor

The astute viewer rejects sharing because saying everyone is equal is groupthink that stokes a race to the bottom.

The knowledgeable viewer argues soft socialists have stopped too many worldwide from becoming wealthy.

The get-ahead viewer laments not knowing wealth accrues by taking from others dooms the majority to poverty.

The aspirational viewer proposes training the poor to develop success muscles by shipping them to an island.

The pragmatic viewer recommends making it a TV show with sales paying to feed and shelter the contestants.

The self-made viewer decrees meaningful competition requires the one who develops a winning ethic escape.

The cheering viewer suggests losers be disposed of and a new group flown in to find the next worthy survivor.

Burgers

The billionaire overdoses on cheese burgers passes
out and when he wakes thinks he won the election.

The billionaire strolls the street waving to the crowds
then has a tantrum because he needs great lighting.

The billionaire demands a contest so only someone
who is truly worthy it is able to reach his corner.

The billionaire knows his corner is the best in the
world because he's standing there tweeting progress.

The billionaire can't believe how crazily the world
is behaving now he's the most voted-for ruler ever.

The billionaire is amazed no ruler has been so rulerish
in the history of rulers in a world now entering peak rule.

The billionaire feels queasy throws up tweets news he
did so is fake and orders another round of burgers.

Mystery

The neighbour suspects he's insufficiently mysterious
so decides he needs to take part in a conspiracy.

The neighbour tries to phone the Russian embassy but
they won't answer and next day he doesn't feel well.

The neighbour wakes that night in a sweat remembering
he's actually a member of a CIA black ops kill squad.

The neighbour binges on Jason Bourne movies and looks
for secret messages in the daily newspaper crossword.

The neighbour meets his handler in a park but doesn't
recognise the code words "nappies" and "play centre".

The neighbour climbs onto the roof of a moving train
and gets arrested waiting for the chopper to airlift him.

The neighbour knows they're out to get him but no
matter what they do to him the world will crack first.

Water
[Remembering Guantanamo]

The citizen appreciates great civilisations need water
to keep those who don't like office towers at bay.

The citizen knows New Zealand isn't great because it only
uses water for drinking washing swimming farming.

The citizen eulogises water's greatness in a blog he
writes to alert citizens to the migrating unwashed.

The citizen urges others to recognise their own greatness
so they'll stop letting just any loser live next door.

The citizen watches parents and their innocent children
playing in a park and realises it needs higher fences.

The citizen walks down the supermarket's aisles and is
appalled it stocks food from so many foreign countries.

The citizen goes home looks at his fish pond and
ponders all the great things it could be used for.

Deal

The accountant feels he's at a nadir so spends time
auditing his soul and finds he's down on inner stock.

The accountant carries out a cost-benefit analysis on
owning a soul and decides he needs better hedging.

The accountant signs up to an industry-endorsed self-
help course that reveals his soul has unmined potential.

The accountant learns that exploiting his potential
comes down to crunching the relevant numbers.

The accountant practises 8 ways to utilise 5 methods
to transform his 6 powers in 12 infallible steps.

The accountant is gratified to find he has strengthened
his soul's position on his life's profit and loss sheet.

The accountant signs an output deal with the universe
he knows will pay off bigtime when the world cashes out.

Platform

The poet zooms in from over the horizon screeches
to a halt and stands in the middle of the page panting.

The poet bows and waits for applause but all is quiet
because they have no platform promoting engagement.

The poet's fellow writers inform them they need
a blog a YouTube channel a celebrity endorsement.

The poet contrarily declares the page their platform
and seeks engagement via a new poetic performance.

The poet slides down S backflips over E and balances
X and Y on their forehead but total silence reigns.

The poet goes into a sulk then looks out the window
and sees two enthusiastic fans outside waving.

The poet happily stands in the middle of the page
smiling back and waving smiling waving smiling ...

Daiquiri

The lizard poet detests cute poems so darts his tongue
across the page and slurps down his alter-ego.

The lizard poet leans back on his air mattress and
takes a luxuriously long slug of frozen daiquiri.

The lizard poet exhales a vaped cloud and wonders
if the world is truly ready for reptilian truths.

The lizard poet's unblinking eyes stare past the end
of the infinity pool as he ponders the poet's burden.

The lizard poet levitates above the floating world looks
down and sees what humanity really wants is distraction.

The lizard poet sighs realises this poem is going nowhere
tears out the page and lets the breeze carry it away.

The lizard poet buffs his scaled claws finishes his daiquiri
and broods over his next splendiferous distraction.

Meanwhile . . .

Memoir

I can't say exactly when it started.
I just know that one day I was dragged
backwards into someone else's hallucination
(my parents' my teachers' all those professionally
employed to peer into the limpid souls of the young)
and thereafter whenever I tried to laugh
a bitter sneeze ricocheted round the room
knocking crockery out the window.
For months I struggled against chains I eventually
came to understand were welded from what others
had projected onto me "for my own good".
Of course I rebelled.
I spun like a Sputnik through the school grounds
I was legally required to occupy five days each week.
I stood in the quad watching clouds and ignoring
the bells that demanded I attend class.
I scratched in the corridor and blamed passing
teachers for thoughtlessly giving me their fleas.
I left the paths and knelt beside signs commanding
"Keep off the grass" to peer into small pools of water
wondering what it would be like to live in there.
I spurned my classmates' attempts at casual conversation
and challenged them instead to define "meaningful".
I careened between emotions like a billiard ball
surprised to find itself on the highway
ricocheting between the tires of speeding cars.
For some reason I thought I could shake
the leaves off one hundred year-old oak trees.
Even now I can't believe I expected to fit in.

At last I realised what I needed was to start a quest
the goal of which I found impossible to explain.
But I had to do something!
Yet I wasn't the only one conflicted.
The world was at war with itself.
Each day came news of the latest kills in Vietnam
students marched in Paris San Francisco Rome
soldiers took potshots at protesters against violence
people divided according to the length of their hair.
But the fear that sent our leaders into paroxysms
was that any day now the communists would invade!
My response was to read
Freud Sartre Shakespeare Jung Plato
Jarry Bly Plath Parra Vaclav Dworkin.
I wanted to learn what had gone wrong
with everything.
I read books my classmates had no interest in
my parents and their friends had never heard of
books that lived outside my studies' boundaries.
I leaped fences and raced eagerly down back alleys
thinking that way I could reach the door
in the forgotten shed at the bottom of the garden
peer into the velvet darkness
and extract intimate readings of the human soul.
For a time things went well.
Strangers gave me tips on where to look
books fell off shelves and landed open at my feet
I even felt the day approaching when I would
perceive the wheels that turn everything.
My confidence grew.
It became obvious answers are a function of questions
I clarified the difference between "and" and "but"

I saw suffering as a comma not a full stop
I learned when to shudder and when to blink.
Then everything fell apart.

At first it was a smell like fried onions
that lurked on the periphery of my perception.
But it turned up everywhere.
In the library in cinemas on buses in the street.
It was especially noticeable when I "looked in".
The climax arrived one day between lectures
when lost in thought I let my guard down
and it jumped me inside the cloisters.
I was smothered in an odour so rancid
it knocked me flat on my back.
By now the source of the smell was inarguable.
It was my soul.
Needing remedial action—and fast—I dropped
my mind into a slingshot and flung it as far
from where I was standing as possible.
This is when I gained a reputation for strangeness.
It was understandable but unavoidable
because who can survive long flapping his arms
like a scarecrow while balanced on a razor?
I adopted the strategy of each day choosing
a colour and the moment I saw it on a coat
shopfront or hoarding I walked away.
I discovered how easily offended people are
when you abandon them mid-speech.
But I also found how little I missed.
We live in ponds of repeated ripples.
Next day they spoke the same words in another order.
As a result my mood shifted.

The smell vanished and I breathed more easily
words came back into focus
when the sun rose each morning it was only the sun.
Then came another change.

By now everything was in transition.
The world was bewildered as it processed how
two million could have starved to death in Biafra.
Yet death remained a divertissement to which
everyone was addicted.
Islamists fought Bathists in Syria
Iran's Shah ordered protesters shot in Jelah Square
the Chilean air force bombed its own president
US bombs lit up the Cambodian jungle
and the Red Brigades kidnapped Aldo Moro
eventually leaving his cold body in the back of a car.
(You appreciate this is not a complete list.)
Simultaneously a stuttering fightback began.
Wars were protested vociferously
discrimination critiqued and contested
radical movements of a political cultural ecological
ecumenical racial and sexual nature were founded
institutional race-based biases were confronted
queerness infiltrated the media
feminists stormed the citadels of patrimony.
The over-riding question became whether
the world would kick off its shoes and walk
barefoot into the future all options open
divert into bare-knuckle fighting
or lose momentum and turn up its toes.
The pressure started to tell.
Important people made grammatical errors

confusing "I" with "we" "them" with "other"
and "other" with "threat".
The situation was soon out of control.
I tried to respond but the ground
was shifting beneath my feet.
My head bounced between right and left
up and down forwards and back.
Standing just made it all worse.
And in the confusion I lost my bearings.

It started with the sound of cracking.
The self so meticulously constructed
over two decades fissured.
Jerrymandered facts and figures that my parents
teachers and television autocue readers
had slapped over my identity started to peel
and fall off as I staggered from
one mundane foolishness to the next.
Soon I wasn't just barefoot but half naked
because my old clothing ceased to fit.
Education was no help.
I realised the university was a bowl
its boundaries specified by certain self-imposed
assumptions that sustained "academic objectivity"
but were really a variety of anaemic cabbage
while my professors resembled goldfish swimming
in circles their mouths opening and closing
opening and closing.
I fell into delirium.
I wanted to fly but continued to sink.
I started circumambulating the Globe
seeking poems to give me oxygen but found

too much mumbling too much sturm and saliva.
It soon became clear everyone was as lost as me.
My problem was few considered it a problem.
For a time I felt I was going mad.
That's when the messages began.

Wherever I went I now found messages
at lectures on notice boards in friend's houses
requesting I do inexplicable things
such as stand in a bookshop on one leg and
whistle like a canary down a mine shaft
or harangue commuters at bus stops explaining
in tedious detail how life is an apple not a banana.
I was told to perform handstands and describe
how the world looked from down there.
Once I was even instructed to categorise
the sighs left behind after church services.
I eventually realised my soul was demanding
I become someone else.
What can you do when your own self rebels?
My old books no longer sustained me
and no one understood what I was talking about.
Naturally I made mistakes
seeking clues in the wrong places—
for example chasing my shadow down the aisles
of a haberdashery store as if a needle and thread
could bridge the metaphysical gap that
now yawned between "I" and "am".
Finally I remembered the abandoned garden shed.
Little did I know the price I would pay
for daring to enter that velvet darkness
with so little in my pockets.

Some places you cannot go in a normal state of mind.
I refer not to derangement of the senses
but to chemicals that punch your ticket then
spin off the wheels eject the driver and dump you
well beyond everyday routes.
Thus began an intense period of lysergic visions.
My mind became an isolation tank
and in the darkness tectonic plates shifted.
There is a fine line between delusion and insight
and I didn't always know which side I was on.
But I learned certain intangible facts.
The modern world is an agreement
we are signed up to by our parents at birth
that we ingest via a process of repetitive chewing.
Life is a diaphanous membrane breathing in-out
and we exist by accommodating ourselves to
the membrane's rhythm at the point where
what we want meets what is.
Identity is a by-product that manifests as
we bounce from one interface point to the next.
Stability is not guaranteed.
Perception is an echo chamber resonating with
multitudinous monologues as each of us
attempts to drown what everyone else is saying
so not to disturb our own point-of-view.
And out of sight at the centre of everything
is the mysterious hidden Other.

The visions that initiated these insights
left a permanent mark due to my head
being displaced a handspan sideways.
Ever since it has swayed beside my shoulders

as I walk down the street.
Of course my perceptions became skewed.
Yet that soon proved the least of my problems
because I now felt I was permanently
walking up the down elevator.
It took a sideways glance to appreciate why.
The advantage of a displaced head is
it enabled me to look at myself.
What I saw produced a profound shock.
I was encased in an enormous overcoat!
A hairy damp-smelling mass hung
over my shoulders arms and body
so heavy it felt lined with lead.
The result was excruciating.
Each step and decision I made
every attempt to do something new
was met by the overcoat's opposed inertia.
It inhibited my achieving anything!
Of course I was not alone.
Seated on the bus with fellow passengers
head bobbing beside my shoulders
watching their blanked commuter expressions
I realised we all lived hunched inside constricting
behavioural patterns woven from our attempts
to adjust to life in the human world.
We are fashion victims of our desire to fit in.

By now I was trying to walk on my hands
while carrying out normal conversations.
People politely pretended not to notice
and inside I thought I was doing fine.
But something had to give.

A new set of writers became my advisors
Huxley Lilly Ginsberg Suzuki Blake
Eckhart Brunton Le Guin Castaneda Dick.
After a day spent burrowing too deep
I would walk the streets late at night
past the darkened windows of sleeping houses
while trying to reach up and grab the moon.
Of course I remained empty-handed.
I understood the moon reflects the sun's light
but had no idea what light is
nor where it met the velvet darkness.
If anyone else knew they weren't saying.
Or I didn't understand.
It was while lost in this in-between state
that the world decided to solve its problems
by lacing on its marching boots
and employing ghouls to rename freedom.
Soviet special forces honoured its *Treaty of
Friendship, Cooperation and Good Neighbourliness*
by entering Afghanistan executing its president
and parading its tanks aircraft troops.
The US initiated *Operation Cyclone* providing
free munitions so mujahideen could restore peace.
Out hunting insurgents during *Operation Rescue*
the Salvadoran army accidentally massacred
eight hundred El Mozote villagers.
After a Marxist-Leninist coup in Grenada
led to introducing rights for workers and women
Operation Urgent Fury hastily crushed the threat
preserving the world for democracy.
The Cold War now ramped up so intensely
young Germans feared they would fry

on the front line of a nuclear endgame.
Millions began shallow breathing on the edges
of empire uncertain who to call for help
in case they triggered the fall of bombs.
Tensions climaxed when the US press
headlined a dangerous "Peace Scare".
Pressure was now on the rest of the world
to get serious and catch up.
They proved fast learners.
Aircraft were hijacked in India Indonesia Ireland
Islamic Jihad blew up US army barracks in Beirut
Iranian students took the US embassy hostage
Pan Am Flight 103 exploded over Lockerbie
military coups stabilised Yugoslavia Nigeria Fiji
Indira Ghandi was shot by her Sikh bodyguards
and three thousand later died in anti-Sikh riots
John Lennon was gunned down in New York
the French sank Greenpeace's protest vessel
Rainbow Warrior in my home town of Auckland.
Yet the ultimate surprise was not that
humanity had allowed their overcoated leaders
to create such a dysfunctional world
but that it could have been much worse.
What saved me from despair was the Double.

In the midst of the world's ongoing delirium
my response was to buy a mirror and
spend time each day staring into my face.
I wanted to discover who I really am.
After weeks of blankness I was startled one day
to realise someone was staring back.
And it wasn't me!

Panicked I tried turning my face away
but whatever it was kept my head immobile.
I was caught.
I moved my eyes in circles to break the connection
but the eyes in the mirror bored in.
By now sweat was trickling down my temple
and the recognition dawned that
an entrance to the beyond had reached out to me.
That was when I glimpsed a flicker deep within
my own reflected eyes—the Double.
The Double is a whisper in a darkened hallway
a subtle feeling containing expansive presence
a breath you can't prove you feel yet do.
Far from scary it was liberating.
It confirmed reality comes inbuilt with windows.

Soon after I woke remembering a dream.
I was looking out the window of a train
but instead of houses between the fences
a single tree grew in each yard.
From the branches people hung like pods
upside down and cased in fur.
As I watched one wriggled vigorously
until it broke loose and fell to the ground.
A camel raced past the train's window
up the road and into the yard where
it licked the fallen pod-person's furry case.
The camel's tongue felt warm and invigorating.
This was the start of my career as a poet.
Days later I sat in my room pen in hand
a blank sheet of paper before me
wondering how to describe what is

and pondering where racing camels fit in.
I blanked my mind and waited.
At that moment a yellow tennis ball
bounced across the floor
and rolled to a halt beside my chair.
The ball throbbed quietly like it was breathing
in out ... in out ... in out.
Abruptly the ball expanded to fill the room
and the lines of a poem arrived
demanding they be written down.
First you must find who you are.
Then anything is possible.

Coda

The poet and the Double play tennis.
Each stands on either side of the net.
To the poet the Double is a faint
presence that exists so far away it is
like a dark smudge in a blackout.
To the Double the poet is a shimmering
blend of feelings thoughts and desires
moving very slowly like in a dream.

As the poet and the Double play
the ball makes indentations
in the surface of the floating world
thock! ... thock! ... thock! ... thock!
No one knows who hit the ball first.
The poet feels he strikes and
the ball comes back to him.
The Double perceives swirling
agglomerations of intents
in which rackets ball and net dance
to create a game of striking patterns
that curve through eternity.

The poet has to concentrate hard
focusing all his attention and willpower
to connect with the ball ... thock!
The Double waves languidly
striking the ball ... thock! ...
while casting horoscopes advising
the lost reviewing life plans and

composing missives from beyond
in the form of antipoems
it tosses over the net
anticipating the ball will eventually
strike one and bounce at an odd
angle
causing spectators to double-take
wondering what they just saw.
This occurs ambiguously.

The poet and the Double play tennis.
Cameras used for analysis
focus on the spectators
not on the players
so the hitting back and forth
can only be inferred by watching
the spectator's eyes.
There is much speculation on
whether a ball is actually in play.
This is debated by philosophers
postmodernists clerics the young
and neurologists who argue the game
is an illusion projected by our brain.
As to the question of whether
the ball still goes thock!
when there's no one to hear it—
don't even ask!

In the middle of play the poet
... thock! ... miscues the ball.
The ball rises so high it
vanishes from sight.

Everyone looks up expectantly
waiting to see
where it will come down.
An eon passes
which is actually only the moment that
exists between a heart and its
beat.
Look! Here the ball comes.
It's getting closer.
Any moment now.
Any moment now.
Any ...
        moment ...
                now?

2018: They made it fun

Improving technology and millennials'
changing expectations of work and family
are giving rise to a new office
arrangement—the coliving/coworking space
often on the beach but always far away.
It's like WeWork meets an upgraded hostel
(in paradise) with free coffee fast internet
a kitchen and quiet spaces while supplying
the serendipitous meetings and experiences
today's digital nomads demand.

18-year-old De'Lindsey Dwayne Mack
was shot and killed outside his school.
De'Lindsey had an alternative persona
on his Instagram page which his family
didn't discover until after his death.
A family friend said the teen posted
pictures of himself with money and guns.
"He was a soft kid
who wanted to be hard."

LOOK GOOD FEEL GREAT SPEND LESS
Want to feel great inside and out?
We can help with that.
NOW $14 Essano Facial Regenerating
or SPF15 75ml Moisturiser.
30% off the Essano Rosehip Skin Range.
[If you'd like to unsubscribe from product
promotion emails like this CLICK HERE.]

We asked 1,500 women across the country
what beauty means to them.
Self-confidence makes us beautiful
think 83% as opposed to good looks (34%)
and a great figure (23%) but women
are still being shamed for their looks.
29% admit to experiencing prejudice
because of weight while
77% of black and 63% of Asian women
have experienced racism
compared to 4% of white women.

    Janet 79 widowed twice.
    Not looking to marry again
    just want to date nice gentleman
    close to my age.
    I hold a black belt in Tae Kwon Do
    and am training in Judo.
    I know how to defend myself.
    So no perverts.

In his new book *Bullshit Jobs: A Theory*
David Graeber is interested in a
particular variety of work and bullshit.
A bullshit job is a form of paid work
that is so completely pointless even
employees cannot justify its existence.
In contrast shit jobs serve a purpose
but suck.
Graeber notes bullshit is widespread.
In one instance a museum guard's job

was to protect an empty room
to ensure no one set it on fire.

Billionaires made more money in 2017
than in any year in recorded history.
The past 30 years have seen far greater
wealth creation than even the Gilded Age
according to the UBS Billionaires 2018 report.
"That period bred generations of families
in the US and Europe such as the Vanderbilts
and Rockefellas and who went on
to influence business banking politics
philanthropy and the arts for over 100 years."
The number of ultra-wealthy people
is growing fastest in China where
two new billionaires are minted each week.

You likely don't spend much time thinking
about your home's lighting.
But it's important.
Besides setting the mood in every room
the way you control your lighting
affects the environment and your bills.
You could pick up any old light switch timer
at the hardware store
but new technology has made
those analog options obsolete.
The Meross Smart WiFi Wall Light Switch
uses voice control and smart home
assistance to take your lighting
out of the dark ages.

Needed quick! Date to family reunion.
Three days all expenses paid.
Looking for man who is 30–45
tall healthy and smart.
Must be comfortable with strangers
able to play endless hours of frisbee
and not a vegetarian.
Must have a good job be either
Christian or willing to pretend
and like animals and kids.
Please be well-groomed too.
Ironed clothes are a big plus.
I am a 31 y.o. athletic
brown-eyed brunette.
Don't respond if you don't think
you can pretend to be my boyfriend.

The biological annihilation of wildlife
means the sixth mass extinction
in Earth's history is under way.
Humanity has wiped out 60% of birds
mammals fish and reptiles since 1970.
The vast and growing consumption of
food and resources by the global population
is destroying the web of life
billions of years in the making.
"Nature is not a nice-to-have" says
Mike Barrett of World Wildlife Fund.
"It's our life-support system.
We are sleepwalking towards
the edge of a cliff."

In three years 145 land and environmental
defenders died in Brazil.
Many were killed attempting to combat
illegal logging in the Amazon.
The Philippines comes second with 102.
Honduras remains the most dangerous
country to be a defender with more killings
per capita than anywhere else.
Industry is driving this violence.
The most deadly industries to go up
against are agribusiness and mining
followed by poaching logging and dams.

The report by the UN Intergovernmental
Panel on Climate Change sent a
psychological shockwave across the planet.
We have only 12 years to enact
"rapid far-reaching and unprecedented
changes in all aspects of society."
That's 12 years to avoid entering an era
marked by severe and regular drought
flooding hurricanes extreme temperatures
mass dislocation and death.

Start your day on beautiful white beaches
and finish watching the sun set over
the emerald waters of the Gulf of Mexico.
With 80 feet of beach frontage
and breathtaking unobstructed views
this almost half acre lot is a rare find.
There are no HOA regulations

so you can remodel the "as is" home
or build your own perfect dream house.

    62 widowed once
    divorced twice.
    Seeking man 60-72
    who looks 50-55.
    No long hair facial hair
    tattoos piercings kids debts
    serious health conditions
    or mental disorders.
    Bikers preferred.

The monetization of identity defines
the ultimate tech business model.
All modern smartphones have inbuilt
GPS accurate to within a few feet.
If Wi-Fi and GPS are turned off
your phone and its apps can use
triangulation of your cell signal
to track where you are.
These technologies were not sold
under the auspices of spyware.
Yet the tradeoff is we have
opened ourselves up to be surveilled
tracked and monitored 24/7
by either companies or governments.

Seven NZ government departments have not
acted in accord with the State Services
Code of Conduct while engaging TCIP

a spy agency that acted unlawfully.
Victims of their covert spy operations
include state abuse survivors iwi
animal rights and climate activists
and opposition political parties.

Some of China's smartest students have been
recruited from high school to train
as the world's youngest AI weapons scientists.
The 27 boys and 4 girls all aged 18
and under were selected for
the 4-year experimental programme
to develop intelligent weapons systems.
China is in competition with
the US and other nations in the race
to develop deadly AI applications
from nuclear submarines with
self-learning chips
to microscopic robots that can crawl
into human blood vessels.
How do you detect submarines
in an expanse as large as the ocean?
The U.S. military hopes to genetically
engineer common marine microorganisms
into living tripwires to tag enemy subs.
It's one potential military application for
the field of synthetic organisms that promises
self-healing paint and biological coatings
that react to their surroundings
and so avoid detection by the enemy.
"Task Force Ocean is about getting us back
to a competitive stance in ocean science."

SW looking for solid relationship.
I am 32 college educated
smart fun and sexy.
I am seeking a man
who is ready to commit.
You must be between
the ages of 30 and 45 and
meet these requirements.
You must own your own home.
You must have a steady job.
You must have your own automobile.
You must be single.
You must not have any kids.
You must not have any pets.
You must enjoy reading.
You must be healthy.
You must not do drugs.
You must not have a criminal record.
You must be willing to respect me.
You must be well-groomed.
Looking a little like Brad Pitt
would be a big plus in your favour.

15 year-old Greta Thunberg describes herself
as a climate radical and is protesting
outside Sweden's parliament every day
until the election calling on politicians
to take climate issues seriously.
"The more you read the more concerned
you get—but instead of worrying
I think you should try to change it."

Human rights organisations are facing
their biggest crackdown in a generation
as a wave of countries pass
restrictive laws to curtail activity.
Almost half the world's states
have implemented controls that affect
organisations across the globe.
The Carnegie Endowment observes
"You can see the protest space shrinking."

Using humor and pop culture savviness
Serbian university students founded
Otpor and sparked a revolution.
Otpor overhauled the image of political
activism to appeal to Generation X's
young and disaffected.
Rejecting violence they aimed for
a revolution of the mind.
In place of weapons they fought with
logos slogans and street theatre.
They used laughter to make resistance
enjoyable corporate-marketing tactics
(a bold logo a memorable slogan)
to make it attractive and technology
to disseminate information and organise.
Simply put—they made it fun.

The poet as agony aunt

Dear Aunty Poet, I'm disillusioned with dating apps. Their recommends just don't work for me. But I want to meet the right one. Do you have any advice? Lovelorn.

> Dear Lovelorn—
> Big data concludes finding love
> ultimately comes down to numbers.
> Many treat dating like buying a ticket
> in Saturday night Lotto
> although they know the odds
> of scoring a winning date are equivalent
> to being bitten by a shark.
> We support the popular alternative
> of kissing an awful lot of frogs.
> Consider accepting webbed feet.

Dear Aunty Poet, My parish priest is a keen gardener. He has invited me to visit his house and view his Bower of Delight, which he says is a garden filled with many different flowers' scents. Being with him makes me glow. Then I think of what others will say, particularly my husband. Should I go? Confused.

> Dear Confused—
> The priest directs us at the heavens
> but his feet remain on the ground.
> You say his words cause you to glow
> yet your life remains a question mark.
> Pick up that question mark

use it to sweep away life's incidentals
then hang it in the closet.
Does it extend down to the floor?
Or is it so small it is hardly visible?
Has it dripped dry?
Does it need starch?
What does it lack that you
are considering the priest's offer?
And what might you lose if he
leads you up the garden path?
There comes a time in life when
these questions must be asked.
Remember you have other options.
Try opening the door in your
shadow and stepping through.

Dear Aunty Poet, I always wanted a husband and children and now I have them so why aren't I happy? I know I can't have everything, but I see other people's houses and look at their lives on Instagram and get jealous. I feel like I'm living at the bottom of a hole and can't get out. Depressed.

Dear Depressed—
The modern world has no interest
in whether you are happy or fulfilled.
To businessmen you are a consumer
they want to continue spending
because they live by taking a cut.
Then when you spend all you have
so you and your family can survive
economists berate you for not

investing or saving for retirement.
But for a fee people will help.
To politicians you are a vote they
attempt to seduce at election time.
The rest of the year you are
a problem they want to go away.
For your boss you are an entry
in the debit column of his
company's weekly accounts.
And deliberately or not friends
pressure you to achieve a lifestyle
that looks good in selfies
but is only possible with money.
Everyone else is unaware you exist.
Naturally you feel empty.
Being left out is a feeling widely
shared in the modern world.
Despite social Darwinists' claims
life is not a competition.
Consider joining a group
whose activities you enjoy.
Focus on being present within.
Do not discount your angst but
don't feed it via negative thinking.
Take time out to watch clouds
form and unform high in the sky.
Stay alert for butterflies.

Dear Aunty Poet, Recently my mother's been telling me social media has taken over my life. But I connect with all my friends through my phone. I have wondered about a digital detox, but what if I don't like it? Uncertain.

Dear Uncertain—
Whatifs sit piled at the intersection where
Maybe Could Have and Didn't meet.
Beyond the intersection is
the park of That Could Be Fun.
Off it is Lonely Street and
the surprises of Lollypop Lane.
Sometimes you just need to pull on
your shoes and start walking.

Dear Aunty Poet, When I wake each morning waves of anxiety pulse through my body. I am anxious about work, that I'll make a mistake or offend someone. I'm especially anxious I'll upset my friends. Sometimes it's so bad I can't eat. My girlfriend says I should be on medication. But is that really what I need? Yes I'm Bovvered.

Dear Yes I'm Bovvered—
Welcome to the modern world!
This won't help you feel better
but at least you are not alone.
Your mind is not your friend.
It has been invaded.
Pills to disrupt thinking reduce anxiety
but feeling inadequate will continue.
You live in a tangle of energy threads
whose vibration is your mind's chatter.
Listen carefully beyond the chatter
and you'll hear marketeers
whispering cynics sniggering
and unhappy colleagues muttering.

None of this is directed at you.
It is the world's neural static.
The world's default setting is send
not receive.
For a cure we suggest the following.
When you wake each morning
take time to look in the mirror.
Set a goal of perceiving the threads
that extend from you into the world.
After a time you'll see the threads
are tethered to an overcoat
you didn't realise you are wearing.
After the initial shock you may think
you like the way it hangs
that you feel secure wearing it.
However comforting these perceptions
your overcoat entangles you
in a behaviourial feedback loop.
The more anxiety you exude the more
reasons to be anxious you receive.
Cut the loop by no longer wondering
what others think of you.
Because they are not thinking of you.
They are caught up in their own overcoat's
threaded thoughts and feelings.
Yet no one *is* their overcoat.
Stare long enough into the mirror
and you will see people walking
as an uncoated glow.
In that light your anxiety will dissolve.
This will take time to achieve.
Do not die wondering.

Dear Aunty Poet, I've lately had a series of bizarre dreams. In one I was my father's father. In another I was married to my mother. Another time I was flying free as a bird, then I turned into a man and was running from people who wanted to kill me. In several dreams I was tortured or falling. I also have erotic dreams involving people I don't know. All these dreams are vivid and disturbing. Sometimes I have the weird feeling they're telling me something. But what? Curious.

Dear Curious—
A Chinese sage once dreamed
he was a butterfly.
When he woke he didn't know
if he was a man dreaming
he was a butterfly or a butterfly
dreaming he was a man.
The dream world hovers
between us and the beyond.
We're told dreams are fantasies.
Yet some dreams are more vivid
than daily experience.
People are alive in the dream world.
Perhaps they're butterflies.
They may or may not be you.
Trying to box dreams into
a this-is-what-they-are explanation
wastes the opportunity they offer.
Curiosity is an assert.
Can you hear a Chinese gong
sounding far in the distance?

It's been struck by a butterfly wing.
When the butterfly's wings flap
ripples spread across the world
causing a storm in your heart.
Both heart and storm are real.
Can anyone then claim
the dream butterfly is not?
Perhaps this world is the dream
and we are in the beyond causing
the butterfly's wings to flap
and stir the ripples of a life?
The dream world is waiting.
In it are clouds of butterflies.
How curious are you?

Dear Aunty Poet, I live in a world where what I am is not what I should be. I'm not white, not male, not female, not religious, not atheist, not privileged, not rich, not good looking, not not not. Wherever I go there's this malevolence directed at me. It's almost physical it's so intense. I appreciate that negative attitudes become internalised and institutionalised. I know people get so fearful and insecure they reject what they don't understand. Of course, for my own safety I could just hang out with people like me. But then I'm ghettoised. Yet if I try to live like everyone else I'm hated. What's the point of being human? What's the point of being alive? Thinking About It.

Dear Thinking About It—
Everyone hears snarling dogs fight
in the street outside their house.

For you the dogs are in the kitchen
showing their teeth.
Understandably this makes
eating breakfast difficult.
But it offers you the insight that
many people are themselves dogs
seated at the breakfast counter
in their own kitchens
snarling at those they don't like.
As you stated snarling is a sign
of fear and insecurity.
The modern world is full of snarling.
The question is how to deal with it.
Being human is an honour.
Yet many reduce the opportunity
to acting like a snarling dog.
Who is the lesser human being
you or them?
And who needs the greater help
you or them?
Wisdom is garnered through
resolving difficulties.
The opportunity for you is
to model the attitudes snarling
dogs need to become human.
This is important work.
The dogs will gradually
be reduced to mere yapping
and will finally eat from
the hands humanity holds out.
You can conquer the world

one snarling dog at a time.
No one would think this not worth
your life's effort.
Be who you need to be.

Dear Aunty Poet, I finish school soon and have decided to become a poet. However, my parents want me to enter a profession. We've had lots of boring talks about it but I know what I want. What I don't know is how to become a poet. How did you start out? What courses do you recommend? Budding Poet.

Dear Budding Poet—
At the risk of being boring
poetry may feed the soul
but it puts no food on the table.
Poets who do not eat die.
Being a dead poet at the start
of your career is less productive
than at its end.
As for how a poet's powers blossom
no two flower the same
so notes from my autobiography
will not benefit you.
Recommended courses are dowsing
flower arranging scuba diving
first aid travel writing studying for
the priesthood and yodelling.
Walking the streets wearing an orange
wig may produce startling insights.
Or not.

My own most memorable lesson
has been learning that words
emerge from the silence which
bubbles in the velvet darkness.

Dear Aunty Poet, I don't know where my life is going. At work I'm bullied by overseers who are bullied by managers who are always on about productivity. The rich get richer. Poverty is huge. We're threatened by pollution and climate change. Television distracts us from realising how big a mess the world is in. And reading just makes me feel worse. Is there a remedy? My Head's Spinning

Dear My Head's Spinning—
You plant your feet one after
the other after the other as you
walk through the world.
Look away from your feet
and observe your shadow.
Your shadow is always there
even when the lights go out.
Your shadow can't get hassled.
Your shadow doesn't complain.
Your shadow is never depressed.
It hasn't ever been distracted or lost.
Become a shadow.

Post-mortem

Now you've done it.
You can never go back.
Yet perhaps while sequestered
within these pages you picked up
some useful life skills such as
how to bbq while nonchalantly
taking a bat to the ghouls climbing
over the fence and sending them
spiralling back into the street ...
riding an e-scooter into the future
while a meta-app updates your soul ...
watching your shadow jump off
a passing Uber and slouch towards you ...
putting your head through the mirror
to discover what's on the other side ...
climbing onto the roof and
joyously howling at the moon ...

The studious are advised to put an x
beside whichever applies.
The competitive are challenged to list
everything they have done better.
The bewildered are requested to call
noise control and complain about
the party in the back of their head.
Everyone else should check their inbox
to see if the universe has sent fresh jokes.

Acknowledgements

References

In poetry everything is permitted ...
Quoted from the poem *Jóvenes (Young Poets)* by Nicanor Parra, translated by Miller Williams, published in Poems & Antipoems (Jonathan Cape, 1968), pg 113.

What the poet had to say during about his apprenticeship ...
Written in 1975, and published that year in *Te Maarama*, Auckland University Student Association's literary magazine.

2001: I would like to meet you
This is a found work, with texts excerpted from newspaper articles published from 1999 to 2001. No record was retained of authors' names or where the pieces were originally published.

2018: They made it fun
This work also consists of found texts, sourced as follows:

Improving technology and millennials' changing ...
Excerpted from *Millennials Are Changing Remote Work*, written by Alexander Besant, posted online by LinkedIn during 2018.

18-year-old De'Lindsey Dwayne Mack ...
Excerpted from *A big talker, but he wasn't a gangster*, a news article written by Courtney Carpenter, posted online by CW39 Houston, 19 November 2018.

LOOK GOOD FEEL GREAT SPEND LESS ...
From a Countdown supermarket email, 11 December 2018.

We asked 1,500 women ...
All statistics are drawn from *Here's what 'beauty' really means*

to women today, an article written by Ali Pontany, based on a survey of reader attitudes, posted online by Glamour Magazine, 1 March 2018.

Janet 79 widowed twice ...
From a selection of personal ads found online by Jayme Kinsey, posted with the heading *Weird and Funny Singles Ads by Women on the Hunt*, on www.pairedlife.com, 20 March 2018.

In his new book *Bullshit Jobs: A Theory* ...
Excerpted from *Looking Busy: The rise of pointless work*, a news article written by Michael Robins on David Graeber's book, posted online by The Nation, December 3-10 issue, 2018.

Billionaires made more money in 2017 ...
From *World's billionaires became 20% richer in 2017*, report reveals, an article written by Rupurt Neate, posted online by The Guardian, 26 October 2018. This and the other excerpts from Guardian stories used courtesy of Guardian News & Media Ltd: www.theguardian.

You likely don't spend much time thinking ...
Posted on Salon Marketplace, November 2018.

Needed quick! Date to family reunion ...
From personal ads compiled by Jayme Kinsey, posted on www.pairedlife.com, 20 March 2018.

The biological annihilation of wildlife ...
Edited from three articles written by Damien Carrington and Jonathan Watts, published in The Guardian 10 July 2017, and 30 October and 6 November 2018.

In three years 145 land and environment defenders ...
Published by The Guardian in an ongoing record of the killing of environmental activists and protectors, using data collected by Global Witness.

The report by the UN Intergovernmental Panel ...
Compiled from various online news items and reports, including an item written by Robert Raymond, published by Huffpost 14 December 2018, and the UN report on climate change posted https://www.ipcc.ch/sr15/.

Start your day on beautiful white beaches ...
From an online real estate advertisement, Craigslist.

62 widowed once ...
From personal ads compiled by Jayme Kinsey, posted on www.pairedlife.com, 20 March 2018.

The monetization of identity defines ...
From *A People's History of Silicon Valley: How the Tech Industry Exploits Workers, Erodes Privacy and Undermines Democracy*, written by Keith Spencer, posted online by Salon, November 11 2018.

Seven government departments ...
Excerpted from an opinion piece written by Dr Russel Norman, formerly co-leader of the NZ Green Party, currently Executive Director of Greenpeace Aotearoa New Zealand, published online www.stuff.co.nz, 19 December 2018.

Some of China's smartest students ...
From a news article posted online in South China Morning Post, 8 November 2018.

How do you detect submarines ...
From an article written by Patrick Tucker, published online by Defense One, 1 December 2018: www.defenseone.com.

SW looking for solid relationship ...
From personal ads compiled by Jayme Kinsey, posted www.pairedlife.com, 20 March 2018.

15 year-old Greta Thunberg describes herself ...
From an article written by Catherine Edwards, posted online by The Local, 24 August 2018.

Human rights organisations are facing ...
Excerpted from *Human rights groups face global crackdown not seen in a generation* written by Harriet Sherwood, published online by The Guardian, 26 August 2015.

Using humour and pop culture savviness ...
Excerpted from *Tracing the Tactics of 21st-Century Youth Protest* by Emma Garland, posted online by Vice, 16 October 2018.

A Tribute

I first discovered Nicanor Parra's poetry in 1974, when I came across *Poems & Antipoems*, (London: Jonathan Cape, 1968), consisting of English translations of work selected from Parra's first four collections. I found the book in Auckland's famed Cook Street Market, buried under remaindered books piled in a cardboard box. Other books I bought at that time included plays by the Czechs Václav Havel and Slawomir Mrozek, prose poems by Charles Baudelaire, *Twenty Love Poems and a Song of Despair* by Pablo Neruda, and Alfred Jarry's dazzling *The Supermale*. All educated me to how writers far from suburban New Zealand viewed the complications of being human.

I found Nicanor Parra's poetry joyously disrespectful. His concept of the antipoem, in tandem with the writing of the American surrealist, Philip Lamantia, pushed me to explore non-naturalistic styles, which led to the writing of *What the poet had to say during his apprenticeship*. But in those days I was more interested in exploring than stopping in one place, so I immediately moved on to try other modes and styles.

Yet of all my youthful work, *What the poet had to say* was an anomaly that I kept coming back to. Periodically, I mulled the idea of writing more poems in the same vein. In July 2018, the idea became an urge. Four months later, with the book well under way, I discovered Nicanor Parra had died a few months earlier, in January.

Accordingly, this collection is written not just as a fulfilment of my long-standing intention to write in Parra's style, but is offered in tribute to the maestro, the inspiration he continues to offer, and the unique body of work he left behind.

Remembering Nicanor Parra

In Santiago Chile the days
are days like everyone's days
the years are years like
everyone else's years
but each moment is a light bulb
only a maestro could transform
into a butterfly zig-zagging crazily
through the halls of high culture
alighting briefly to paddle
in a pool of blood dripping
from the nose of the President
of PEN International
then flying into the scrollery
to make jagged marks
on pristine parchment pages
which are caught in a breeze
that lifts them through the window
and scatters them serendipitously
across the whole floating world.

To the reader

Small presses rely on the support of readers to tell others about the books they enjoy. To support this book and its author, we ask you to consider placing a review on the site where you bought it. For more on Keith Hill and his books, and sign up to his newsletter: www.keithhillauthor.com. Keith Hill's other poetry includes:

The Ecstasy of Cabeza de Vaca

""A tour de force. Hill's humanizing of de Vaca is the ingredient that makes it so moving and once taken up, impossible to put down."
— Alistair Paterson
"An extraordinary effort of imagination. In New Zealand literature there's no one quite like Keith Hill, and certainly no long poem like this one." —Roger Horrocks

Out of the Way World Here Comes Humanity!

"Up-to-the-minute reportage on our fraught zeitgeist, conveyed with vitality and satirical humour." — Hugh Major
"Pertinent to some of the world's biggest challenges. A thought-provoking and incredibly poignant read for anyone grappling with the climate crisis." — Alva Feldmeier, Executive Director, 350 Aotearoa

Interpretations of Desire: Mystical love poems by Ibn 'Arabi

"The *Tarjumán al-Aswáq* is one of the greatest works of Islamic mystical poetry. Keith Hill's artful and beautiful renditions will bring Ibn 'Arabi's neglected masterpiece to a new readership."
—Nile Green, author of *Sufism: A Global History*

The Bhagavad Gita: A new poetic translation

"An enthralling new rendering, which balances spiritual insight, poetic power and philosophic accuracy." —Peter Calvert, co-author of *The Kosmic Web*

Psalms of Exile and Return

"In a time that is spiritually dry for so many, this book of psalms is water in the desert. They challenge, terrify, comfort, and call us to a deep humanity." — Allan Jones, Dean Emeritus, Grace Cathedral, San Francisco

I Cannot Live Without You: Selected poems of Mirabai and Kabir

"Reminded me it's been an eternity since I was hungry for God. This book will renew your hunger for your sacred flame." —Judith Hoch PhD, author of *Prophecy on the River*

www.ingramcontent.com/pod-product-compliance
Lightning Source LLC
Chambersburg PA
CBHW030452010526
44118CB00011B/902